A GUIDE TO THE JOSEPH SMITH PAPYRI

A
GUIDE
TO THE
JOSEPH SMITH
PAPYRI

JOHN GEE

The Foundation for Ancient Research and Mormon Studies (FARMS)
at Brigham Young University
Provo, Utah

Design by Bjorn W. Pendleton

John Gee (Ph.D., Yale University) is assistant research professor of Egyptology
at FARMS and research associate for the Center for the Preservation of Ancient
Religious Texts (CPART) at Brigham Young University.

The Foundation for Ancient Research and Mormon Studies (FARMS)
at Brigham Young University
P.O. Box 7113
University Station
Provo, Utah 84602

Library of Congress Cataloging-in-Publication Data

Gee, John.
A guide to the Joseph Smith papyri / by John Gee.
p. cm.
Includes bibliographical references and index.
ISBN 0-934893-54-3
1. Book of Abraham. 2. Egyptian language—Papyri, Hieroglyphic. I.
Title
BX8629.P5 G44 2000
289.3'2—dc21
00-009956

*C*ontents

*I*llustrations

*A*cknowledgements

This publication would not have been possible without the assistance of several individuals. Without the encouragement and support of M. Gerald Bradford, the director of research at the Foundation for Ancient Research and Mormon Studies, this publication would never have seen the light of day. Clark Gee, Brian M. Hauglid, Matthew Roper, Brian L. Smith, John A. Tvedtnes, and my wife, Kathleen, have provided important feedback. Wendy H. Christian, Alison V. P. Coutts, and Angela Clyde of the FARMS editorial staff have been unfailingly helpful in preparing the manuscript for publication. I would also like to thank Carmen Cole for helping make the charts readable; Julie A. Dozier, Paula W. Hicken, Linda M. Sheffield, and Sandra A. Thorne for proofreading the manuscript; Rebecca Sterrett for producing the maps; and Bjorn Pendleton for designing the volume. My sincere appreciation also goes to the Church of Jesus Christ of Latter-day Saints for permission to publish pictures of the Joseph Smith Papyri and the Kirtland Egyptian Papers, which reside in their archives, and to whom the intellectual property rights of these materials belong.

Egypt in Greco-Roman Times

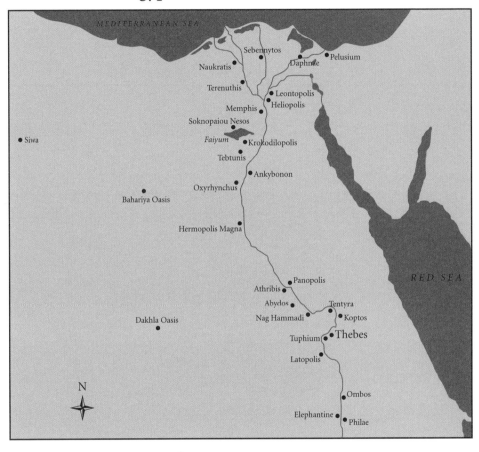

*I*ntroduction

More than a dozen years of answering questions about the Joseph Smith Papyri on a weekly, if not daily, basis have convinced me that one of the major problems with understanding the complicated issues surrounding the papyri has been the lack of up-to-date, reliable, readily available information on the Joseph Smith Papyri. Many discussions of the papyri are often completely devoid of not only recent Egyptological research but sometimes of even basic information about ancient Egypt. Additionally, few of the available discussions show any acquaintance with serious Latter-day Saint thought on either the Book of Abraham or the Joseph Smith Papyri. This guide has been prepared to provide basic information about the Joseph Smith Papyri and an overview of the discussion about the connections that they may have with the Book of Abraham for those who have no knowledge of ancient Egypt and perhaps little of the Latter-day Saints.

Due to the general nature of this work, references have been kept to an absolute minimum. I am currently preparing a larger study that will provide a fuller discussion with references.

The present work is not an official publication of the Church of Jesus Christ of Latter-day Saints and does not necessarily represent the official positions of the Church of Jesus Christ of Latter-day Saints, Brigham Young University, or the Foundation for Ancient Research and Mormon Studies at Brigham Young University.

Joseph Smith Papyrus I (in current condition). The vignette is the original of Facsimile 1 of the Book of Abraham. The hieroglyphs on the right give the name, titles, and genealogy of Hor, the original owner of the manuscript.

1

Historical Overview

Early History of the Papyri

In the early part of the nineteenth century, Antonio Lebolo, an antiquities dealer working under the consul general of Egypt, plundered several tombs in Thebes in southern Egypt. Some of the antiquities he sold; others he kept. Among those he kept were eleven mummies that he brought home to Italy.

After Lebolo's death, his family sent the mummies through the shipping company of Albano Oblasser to sell in America to the highest bidder. The highest bidder was Michael Chandler, who, having failed to find valuables inside the mummies other than some papyri, took them around as part of a traveling curiosity show. After two years on the road, Chandler's mummy show reached Kirtland, Ohio, then

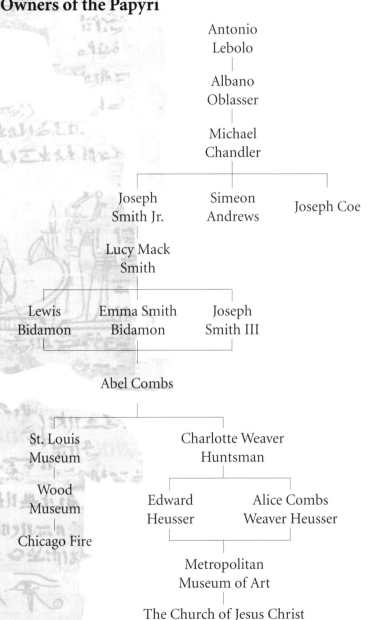

Owners of the Papyri

Antonio
Lebolo

Albano
Oblasser

Michael
Chandler

Joseph
Smith Jr.   Simeon
                         Andrews   Joseph Coe

Lucy Mack
Smith

Lewis   Emma Smith   Joseph
Bidamon   Bidamon   Smith III

Abel Combs

St. Louis   Charlotte Weaver
Museum   Huntsman

Wood   Edward   Alice Combs
Museum   Heusser   Weaver Heusser

Chicago Fire

Metropolitan
Museum of Art

The Church of Jesus Christ
of Latter-day Saints

the headquarters of the fledgling Church of Jesus Christ of Latter-day Saints.[1]

Joseph Smith, prophet of the church, examined the several papyrus rolls and, after commencing "the translation of some of the characters or hieroglyphics," said that "one of the rolls contained the writings of Abraham, another the writings of Joseph of Egypt, etc."[2] In early July of 1835, Joseph Coe, Simeon Andrews, Joseph Smith, and others paid Chandler $2400 for four mummies and at least five papyrus documents, including two or more rolls[3] (see charts on pages 10–13).

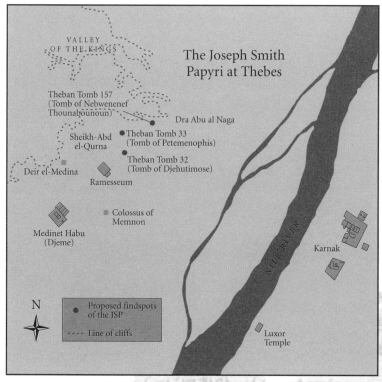

Several locations where Antonio Lebolo could have found the Joseph Smith Papyri are indicated.

History of the Translation of the Book of Abraham

Joseph Smith began translating the papyri in early July 1835. The current text of the Book of Abraham was translated by the end of the month. He left off translation in August 1835 to visit the Saints in Michigan.[4] Revelation pertaining to the Book of Abraham was not received again until 1 October 1835.[5] Translation continued through 25 November 1835, but Joseph then set aside the papyri to study Hebrew, finish the Kirtland temple and dedicate it, and, later, deal with troubles in Missouri. While Joseph slightly revised the translation preparatory to its publication in 1842, there is no other evidence that he worked on the translation of the existing Book of Abraham after 1835 (see chart on opposite page).

We have no firsthand evidence that Joseph Smith used the Urim and Thummim or a seer stone in translating the Book of Abraham. Nor did Joseph apparently use any grammars or dictionaries in preparing his translations. Joseph Smith himself never discussed how he translated the Book of Abraham. Nevertheless, Warren Parrish, one of the scribes involved in the translation during late 1835, stated, "I have set [sic] by his side and penned down the translation of the Egyptian Hieroglyphicks [sic] as he claimed to receive it by direct inspiration of Heaven."[6]

History of the Publication of the Book of Abraham

In early 1842 Joseph Smith, Willard Richards, and Reuben Hedlock prepared the text for publication in the *Times and Seasons*. Only three installments were published, which included about one quarter of what Joseph Smith translated. Unfortunately the location of the original manuscripts of his

Timeline for the Translation and Publication of the Book of Abraham

First Translation Period	**3 July 1835**	Michael Chandler arrives in Kirtland with the mummies.
	6 July 1835	Michael Chandler issues certificate to Joseph Smith about his translation abilities. Some of the Saints in Kirtland purchase mummies.
	July 1835	Joseph Smith translates the Book of Abraham.
Second Translation Period	**1 Oct. 1835**	With Oliver Cowdery and W. W. Phelps, Joseph Smith receives revelation about the system of astronomy (Facsimile 2).
	7 Oct. 1835	Joseph Smith recommences translating the Book of Abraham.
	29 Oct. 1835	Warren Parrish hired as scribe.
	19 Nov. 1835	Translation
	24 Nov. 1835	Translation
	25 Nov. 1835	Translation
	26 Nov. 1835	Translation
Publication Period	**19–26 Feb. 1842**	Type is set for the first installment of the Book of Abraham.
	23 Feb. 1842	Joseph Smith commissions Reuben Hedlock to make cuts to accompany the Book of Abraham in the *Times and Seasons*.
	1 Mar. 1842	First installment of the Book of Abraham is published in the *Times and Seasons* (vol. 3, no. 9, containing Abraham 1:1–2:18 and Facsimile 1).
	4 Mar. 1842	Joseph Smith shows Reuben Hedlock the papyri so he can make the cut for Facsimile 2, illustrating the principles of astronomy.
	8 Mar. 1842	Joseph Smith revises translation of the Book of Abraham.
	9 Mar. 1842	Joseph Smith continues revisions.
	15 Mar. 1842	Second installment of the Book of Abraham is published in the *Times and Seasons* (vol. 3, no. 10, containing Abraham 2:19–5:21 and Facsimile 2).
	16 Mar. 1842	Facsimile 3 of the Book of Abraham is published in the *Times and Seasons*.

translation is presently unknown and thus about three quarters of Joseph Smith's translation of the Book of Abraham is lost. The three facsimiles made to accompany the translation of the Book of Abraham were cut to actual size by Reuben Hedlock.

In 1851 Franklin D. Richards, then the newest apostle of the church and the new president of the European Mission headquartered in England, found that the church members in England—the location with the largest concentration of Latter-day Saints in the world at the time—had almost no church literature. Elder Richards included the Book of Abraham in "a choice selection from the revelations, translations, and narrations of Joseph Smith," published as *The Pearl of Great Price*.[7] It was "not adapted, nor designed, as a pioneer of the faith among unbelievers"; instead it was designed for the Saints to "increase their ability to maintain and to defend the holy faith by becoming possessors of it."[8] The facsimiles of the Book of Abraham were recut with this edition and succeeding editions, becoming increasingly more inaccurate with subsequent editions.

In 1878 the Pearl of Great Price was published in Utah. Two years later it was canonized by a vote of the general conference. The longest-used edition was published in 1907; it had the most inaccurate copies of the facsimiles and continued to be used until the 1981 English edition restored Hedlock's original facsimiles. The 1981 edition has been the standard edition ever since (see chart on opposite page).

Later History of the Papyri

When Joseph Smith bought the papyri, the outer ends of the papyrus scrolls were already damaged. To prevent further

Publication History of the Hypocephalus

Original Reuben Hedlock Engraving
1842 *Times and Seasons*
1981 Edition

1878 Salt Lake City Edition

1907 Salt Lake City Edition
Most Egyptological Publications

1851 Liverpool Edition
1879 Liverpool Edition
1891 Salt Lake City Edition

PURPLE: only in 1842 edition; BLUE: not in 1851 edition;
RED: not in 1878 or 1907 edition; GREEN: not in 1907 edition.

While the original facsimiles of the Book of Abraham were made directly from the papyri, later copies were not and have progressively deteriorated, as illustrated here by Facsimile 2. Lines and figures that are missing from each edition are marked in color. Figures missing from the 1878 edition are also not on the 1907 edition. The illustration does not show distortions in the proportions in various editions.

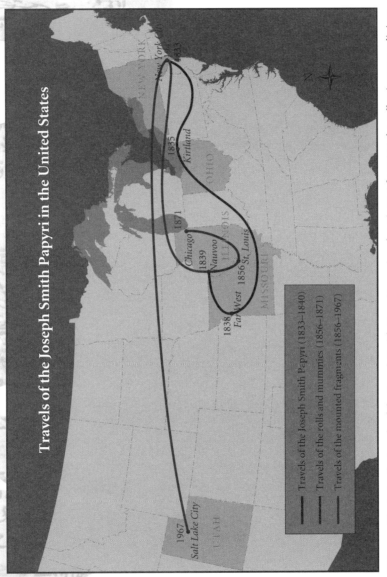

Travels of the Joseph Smith Papyri in the United States

This map illustrates the travels of the Joseph Smith Papyri to various locations. After 1856 the collection was split into two groups. Routes shown are not exact. Only key dates are indicated.

Travels of the Joseph Smith Papyri (1833–1840)
Travels of the rolls and mummies (1856–1871)
Travels of the mounted fragments (1856–1967)

damage, the outside portions of some of the papyri were separated from their rolls, mounted on paper, and placed in glass frames. The remainder of the rolls were kept intact.

In Nauvoo Joseph Smith turned over the mummies and papyri to his mother, Lucy Mack Smith, to free himself from the obligation of exhibiting the papyri and to provide his widowed mother with means to support herself. She kept the mummies and papyri for the rest of her life, exhibiting them to interested visitors for twenty-five cents a person. On 26 May 1856, less than two weeks after Mother Smith died, Emma Smith (Joseph's widow), her second husband, Lewis C. Bidamon, and her son, Joseph Smith III, sold the mummies and the papyri to Abel Combs.[9]

Abel Combs split up the papyri. Some he sold to the St. Louis Museum, including at least two of the rolls and at least two of the mummies; some of the mounted fragments he kept. The St. Louis Museum sold the rolls and mummies to the Wood Museum in Chicago. The Wood Museum burned down in the Chicago Fire of 1871, and presumably the papyri and mummies were destroyed with it. The mounted fragments passed from Abel Combs to the hands of Edward and Alice Heusser. In 1918 Alice Heusser offered the papyri to the Metropolitan Museum of Art in New York. At the time, the museum was not interested. In 1947 Ludlow Bull, the associate curator of the Department of Egyptian Art, purchased the papyri for the Metropolitan Museum from Edward Heusser. On 27 November 1967 the Metropolitan Museum presented the fragments of the papyri to the Church of Jesus Christ of Latter-day Saints. The church published the papyri two months later in the *Improvement Era*;[10] the current numbering system of the papyri derives from this publication. To the disappointment of many, while these remaining fragments contained the original drawing for Facsimile 1, they were not the portion of the papyri that contained the text of the Book of Abraham (see charts on pages 10–13).

An Overview of the Papyri

Document	Known Contents	Estimated Original Dimensions
Papyrus of Hor	Owner's name, titles, genealogy; Facsimile 1 from the Book of Abraham; the Book of Breathings Made by Isis (only 4 of an original 6 columns remain); Facsimile 3; and another text of which only the opening words ("Beginning of the Book of . . .") have been preserved.	13 cm x 320 cm (13 cm x 68 cm is still extant)
Papyrus of Semminis	Book of the Dead chapters 3, 4, 5, 6, 53, 54, 57, 63, 65, 67, 70, 72, 74, 75, 76, 77, 83, 86, 87, 88, 89, 91, 100, 101, 103, 104, 105, 106, 110, 125, and other unidentified texts.	32 cm x 320 or 640 cm (now 32 cm x 117 cm)
Papyrus of Noufianoub	Vignette for the Book of the Dead 125 and other unidentified texts.	32 cm x 320 cm (now 32 cm x 33 cm)
Papyrus of Amenophis	Book of the Dead 45 and other unidentified texts.	32 cm x 320 cm
Hypocephalus of Sheshonq	Facsimile 2 (hypocephalus).	19 cm x 20 cm

* m = male; f = female

That Joseph Smith Owned[11]

Preserved Fragments	Disposition of Fragments	Ancient Owner
JSP I, XI, and X	Outer fragments from the roll remain. The inner portion of the roll, including Facsimile 3, was destroyed in the Chicago Fire of 1871.	Hor (ḥr)[m*], son of Osoroeris (wsir-wr)[m] and Chibois (tꜣy-ḫy-biꜣ.t)[f]
JSP VII, VIII, V, VI, IV, and II. The fragments in JSP IX are scattered throughout.	Some fragments from the roll remain. The inner portion of the roll was probably destroyed in the Chicago Fire of 1871.	Semminis (tꜣ-šr.t-mn)[f], daughter of Eskhons (ns-ḥnsw)[f]
JSP IIIa–b	Unknown; perhaps destroyed in the Chicago Fire of 1871.	Noufianoub (nfr-ir.t-nwb)[f]
None	Unknown; perhaps destroyed in the Chicago Fire of 1871.	Amenophis (imn-ḥtp)[m], son of Tanoub (tꜣ-nwb)[f]
Facsimile 2	Unknown; perhaps destroyed in the Chicago Fire of 1871.	Sesonchis (ššnq)[m]

Original Extent of the Joseph Smith Papyri*

Scroll of Hor

320 cm (about 10 feet)

13 cm

To the Wood Museum in Chicago (1864) and destroyed in the Chicago Fire (1871)

Scroll of Semminis

320 cm

32 cm

← (Early accounts indicate this scroll may have been extended twice as long as shown here in this direction.)

Scroll of Noufianoub

320 cm

32 cm

JSP III

To the Metropolitan Museum of Art (1947) and then the LDS Church (1967)

Scroll of Amenophis

320 cm

32 cm

No fragments of this scroll remain. It is known only from a partial copy.

Hypocephalus of Sheshonq
(original now missing)

JSP X   JSP XI   JSP I

To the Metropolitan Museum of Art
(1947) and then the LDS Church (1967)

JSP II   JSP IV   JSP VI   JSP V   JSP VII

JSP VIII

To the Metropolitan Museum of Art (1947) and then the LDS Church (1967)

*Outlines show estimated original dimensions; pictured fragments indicate exist-
ing papyri in the possession of the Church of Jesus Christ of Latter-day Saints.

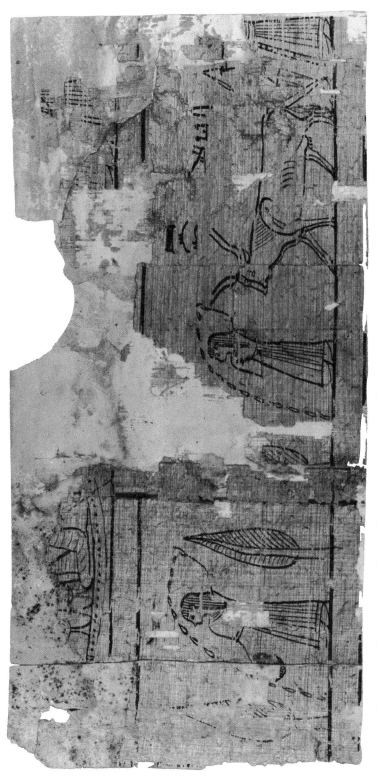

Joseph Smith Papyrus II (in current condition). The vignette is from Book of the Dead 110. A woman named Semminis (late third century B.C.) originally owned the papyrus.

2

The Ancient Owners of the Papyri

From the names, titles, and genealogies written on the papyri, we know their ancient owners were Egyptian priests who lived in Thebes in Egypt. They were wealthy individuals who came from important political families. For example, the father of Hor (the owner of JSP I) was the great governor of Thebes. Their official positions were often hereditary.

The ancient owners of the papyri were among the most literate and educated people of the country. They had access to the great Theban temple libraries, containing narratives, reference works, and manuals, as well as scrolls on religion, ritual, and history. The papyri owners also lived at a time when stories about Abraham are known to have circulated in Egypt. If any ancient Egyptians were in a position to know about Abraham, it was the class of people to whom the owners of the Joseph Smith Papyri belonged.

The Egyptian religion of the time was complex and eclectic. Foreign elements (such as deities and rites), including those from the Greek religion and Judaism, were added to Egyptian practices. As priests, the ancient owners were required to maintain strict standards of personal conduct and purity. Egyptian priests of the time were often buried with a variety of different texts all written on the same papyrus roll, one after the other.

Egyptian Traditions about Abraham

Writer/Text That Mentions Abraham	Ruler/Time Period
Hecataeus of Abdera	Ptolemy I (305–282 B.C.)
Septuagint	Ptolemy II (285–246 B.C.)
Artapanus	Ptolemy V (204–180 B.C.)
Eupolemus	Ptolemy VI (180–145 B.C.)
Testament of Abraham	First century A.D. ?
Philo of Alexandria	Tiberius (A.D. 14–37)
Zosimus of Panopolis	Third century A.D.
Anastasi Archive	Third century A.D.

Joseph Smith Papyrus III (in current condition). The vignette accompanied Book of the Dead 125 in Ptolemaic times (332–30 B.C.). The papyrus originally belonged to a woman named Noufianoub.

3

Theories to Explain
the Book of Abraham

Because we do not have all the papyri that Joseph Smith had, and because those that have been preserved do not contain a copy of the text of the Book of Abraham, there is no simple answer to the question, "Did Joseph Smith translate the Book of Abraham correctly?" Instead, answers are given based on various theories about issues such as (1) the relationship of the Book of Abraham text to the papyri, (2) the date of the Book of Abraham text, (3) the date of the papyri, (4) the transmission of the text, and (5) the nature of the facsimiles. In certain incomplete presentations, many of the conclusions based on the theories may seem valid at first glance. A more careful study of theories concerning the Book of Abraham translation, however, reveals that the theories are often assumed rather than examined or even stated, and thus the conclusions based on them, while sometimes appearing plausible, may be suspect. Below we examine the main theories since there is no single Latter-day Saint or non–Latter-day Saint position on these issues.

Theories about the Book of Abraham

Relation of Book of Abraham to Papyri	Date of Book of Abraham	Date of Papyri	Transmission of Text	Nature of Facsimiles
Kirtland Egyptian Papers Theory	Abrahamic	Abraham's Day	Manuscript written by Abraham	Egyptian funerary texts
Missing Papyrus Theory	Hellenistic	Ptolemaic Period	Abraham wrote text in Egypt and it stayed there	Illustrations of the day
Pure Revelation Theory	Modern	Roman Period	Abraham's descendants brought text to Egypt	Copied from Abraham's drawings
			Mnemonic device used to link two texts	Drawn by Abraham

Relationship of the Book of Abraham Text to the Papyri

Several theories posit ways in which the Book of Abraham text relates to the papyri. These may be categorized as the Kirtland Egyptian Papers theory, the missing papyrus theory, and the pure revelation theory.

Some people, both Mormon and non-Mormon, believe that Joseph Smith used the Kirtland Egyptian Papers (sometimes mistakenly called the Alphabet and Grammar*) to produce the Book of Abraham from the papyri. The Kirtland Egyptian Papers were a group of miscellaneous documents primarily in the handwriting of several men who served at various times as Joseph Smith's scribes, and these documents were produced in Kirtland or Nauvoo. Three of the documents from the Kirtland Egyptian Papers contain a partial copy of the translated Book of Abraham in which a word or two in Egyptian characters is written in the left-hand margin at the beginning of each paragraph of English text. According to this theory, the text to the right is the translation of the Egyptian characters to the left. Unfortunately for this theory, the Egyptian characters were added after the entire English text was written (as evidenced by the use of different inks, Egyptian characters that do not always line up with the English text, and Egyptian characters that sometimes overrun the English text). Thus it was not a matter of writing the character and then writing the translation but of someone later adding the characters in the margin at the beginning of paragraphs of text without explicitly stating the reason for doing so.

---

*There is no document called the "Alphabet and Grammar." Those who use this term use it either to refer to the Kirtland Egyptian Papers or to a specific document among them titled "Grammar and Alphabet of the Egyptian Language."

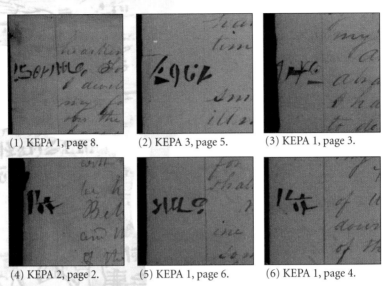

(1) KEPA 1, page 8.   (2) KEPA 3, page 5.   (3) KEPA 1, page 3.

(4) KEPA 2, page 2.   (5) KEPA 1, page 6.   (6) KEPA 1, page 4.

Examples of Egyptian characters written in the margins of the Kirtland Egyptian Papers Book of Abraham manuscripts (KEPA). The examples show that the characters (1) were written in different ink than the English text (examples 2, 3, 4, 6), (2) do not line up with the English text (examples 3, 4, 6), and (3) run over the margins (examples 1, 2, 5) and sometimes the English text (example 1). This indicates that the Egyptian characters were added after the English text was written, perhaps to decorate the beginnings of paragraphs, although the reason for their inclusion was never explicitly stated.

Advocates of the Kirtland Egyptian Papers theory also assume that Joseph Smith first compiled a grammar from which he then produced the translation. But when a text in an unknown language is initially translated, a decipherer usually cracks the language without the use of grammars. Grammarians then go through the translation, establish the grammatical usage, and compile a grammar. Later, individuals learn the grammar and then produce translations. As a decipherer and one who had never formally studied any grammar at the time he produced the translation, Joseph Smith would have done the translation first.

The Kirtland Egyptian Papers that have been connected with the papyri appear to be a later attempt to match up the translation of the Book of Abraham with some of the Egyptian characters (see examples on opposite page). If one assumes that the Book of Abraham was the second text on the papyrus of Hor, a possible scenario is that having the translation of the Book of Abraham, the brethren at Kirtland tried to match the Egyptian characters with the translation but chose the characters from the first text. Yet it is not certain that this is what they thought they were doing.

Some have reasoned that since the preserved papyri account for no more than 13 percent of all the papyri that Joseph Smith possessed, the Book of Abraham does not match the translation of the preserved papyri because it was most likely translated from a portion of the papyri that is now missing. Any theory such as this one that has Joseph Smith translating an authentic ancient text assumes that he did so by divine inspiration.

Others have thought that the Book of Abraham was not connected in any way with the papyri but was received by pure inspiration. Mormons and non-Mormons who hold this theory differ as to the source of that inspiration.

Date of the Text of the Book of Abraham

The date of a text is the date when the text was written by its author. A text can be copied into various manuscripts or translated into other languages, and these manuscripts or translations will have different, later dates than the date of the original text. When we refer to the date of the text, we refer to the date of the original text. For example, the text of the Gospel of Matthew was written in the first century A.D., but

Egyptian Chronology

4500–3150 B.C.	Predynastic Period
3150–2700 B.C.	Early Dynastic Period
2700–2190 B.C.	Old Kingdom
2200–2040 B.C.	First Intermediate Period
2046–1794 B.C.	Middle Kingdom
1795–1553 B.C.	Second Intermediate Period
1552–1069 B.C.	New Kingdom
1295–1069 B.C.	Ramesside Period
1069–702 B.C.	Third Intermediate Period
1069–715 B.C.	Lybian Period
747–656 B.C.	Kushite Period
672–525 B.C.	Saite Period
525–359 B.C.	First Persian Period
404–343 B.C.	Dynasties 27–30
343–332 B.C.	Second Persian Period
332–30 B.C.	Ptolemaic Period
30 B.C.–A.D. 395	Roman Period
A.D. 396–642	Byzantine Period

the earliest manuscript that we have of Matthew was copied in the third century. Theories about the date that the text of the Book of Abraham was written—whether Abrahamic, Greco-Roman, or modern—have characterized the major division between Latter-day Saint and non–Latter-day Saint approaches to the Book of Abraham. The text of the Book of Abraham is usually dated (to modern or ancient times) by assumption rather than by any attempt to demonstrate the milieu out of which it came.

Most non–Latter-day Saints think that the Book of Abraham

is a modern fabrication by Joseph Smith. A handful of Latter-day Saints think that the Book of Abraham was written by an unknown individual in Greco-Roman Egypt (fourth century B.C. through the fifth century A.D.) and that it is an ancient pseudepigraphon translated by Joseph Smith. Most Latter-day Saints believe the text to be written by the patriarch Abraham.

Date of the Papyri

The date of the Joseph Smith Papyri is a separate issue from the date of the text of the Book of Abraham and remains an issue regardless of whether or not the papyri are viewed as the source of the Book of Abraham. The three time periods proposed are Abraham's day, the Ptolemaic period, and the Roman period.

Some have assumed that the papyri date to Abraham's day. This notion is supported by hearsay sources (notably Josiah Quincy) who misunderstood what Joseph Smith said.[12] Those who assume that the papyri date to Abraham's day often do not distinguish between the date of a text and the date of a manuscript, which is a copy of that text. (For example, Paul's letter to the Galatians was written in the first century, but most of the manuscripts date to much later.) This theory is largely a straw man since it is mostly anti-Mormons who claim that Mormons believe that the papyri, rather than the text, date to Abraham's time.

For many years the standard date for the Joseph Smith Papyri was the Roman period, either in the first century B.C. or in the first century A.D. (or more precisely, the second half of the first century A.D.). This was argued on the basis of the hieratic handwriting (a cursive form of ancient Egyptian) on the papyri, sometimes additionally shored up by connecting the

Greco-Roman Egyptian Chronology

332 B.C. Alexander the Great conquers Egypt

305 B.C. Ptolemy I (Soter) becomes Pharaoh

282 B.C. Ptolemy II Philadelphos becomes Pharaoh

247 B.C. Ptolemy III Euergetes becomes Pharaoh

222 B.C. Ptolemy IV Philopator becomes Pharaoh

205 B.C. Thebes revolts under Haronnophris
     Ptolemy V Epiphanes becomes Pharaoh

199 B.C. Chaonnophris succeeds Haronnophris

197 B.C. Rosetta Stone Decree issued

187 B.C. Ptolemy V finally defeats Chaonnophris

181 B.C. Ptolemy VI Philometer becomes Pharaoh

c. 181–170 B.C. Jewish temple erected in Leontopolis

170 B.C. Ptolemy VIII Euergetes II begins rule as coregent

146 B.C. Ptolemy VIII assumes sole rule

132–131 B.C. Thebes revolts under Hariese

117 B.C. Ptolemy IX Soter II becomes Pharaoh

81 B.C. Ptolemy XII Auletes becomes Pharaoh

52 B.C. Cleopatra VII Philopator becomes ruler of Egypt

30 B.C. Caesar Augustus becomes ruler of Egypt

A.D. 14 Tiberius rules Egypt

A.D. 40 Claudius rules Egypt

A.D. 54 Nero rules Egypt

A.D. 63 Demotic Book of the Dead

A.D. 68 Vespasian rules Egypt

A.D. 71 Jewish Temple at Leontopolis closes

A.D. 78 Titus rules Egypt

A.D. 81 Domitian rules Egypt

A.D. 97 Trajan rules Egypt

A.D. 107 Soter archon in Thebes

A.D. 116 Hadrian rules Egypt

papyri with the Soter find,* an early second-century A.D. cache also excavated by Antonio Lebolo.

More recently, Egyptologists have dated the Joseph Smith Papyri to the Ptolemaic period, more specifically to the first half of the second century B.C. or late third century B.C. They support their arguments by identifying those who originally owned the papyri as the same individuals mentioned in dated sources by means of their priestly titles and family associations. Those who have argued for this date have pointed out that hieratic handwriting is an unreliable criterion for the Ptolemaic and Roman periods and that none of the individuals in the Soter find are related to anyone mentioned in the Joseph Smith Papyri.

Transmission of the Text

Those who believe that the original text of the Book of Abraham dates back to Abraham himself can also be further distinguished by four different theories of textual transmission. (Textual transmission is the means by which the text was passed down, or transmitted, through time.)

Those who believe that the manuscript (and not just the text) of the Book of Abraham dates back to Abraham's day think the papyri were written by Abraham while he was in Egypt; thus textual transmission does not occur in this theory. Although anti-Mormons often attribute this belief to Latter-day Saints, there is nothing in the teachings of the church that compels this conclusion nor is it a universally held belief among Latter-day Saints.

A second theory holds that Abraham wrote the text of the

---

*Soter was the governor of Thebes in A.D. 107.

Book of Abraham as an Egyptian text while he was in Egypt, that the text was then transmitted by Egyptians, and that the papyri are a later manuscript. Proponents of this view do not take into account why, if it were intended for Egyptians, there are explanations of Egyptian customs and beliefs in the text. The Book of Abraham seems to be directed toward an audience unfamiliar with Egyptian customs (see, for example, Abraham 1:21–27).

A third theory of transmission postulates that the Book of Abraham was written by Abraham and passed down through his descendants (the Jews), some of whom took a copy to Egypt where it was copied (after being translated) onto a later manuscript.

Another more complicated theory of textual transmission is called the mnemonic device theory. Supporters of this theory hypothesize that the Egyptian characters could serve as a sort of mnemonic device for ancient scribes to recall the Book of Abraham as well as to convey the Egyptian text. This way someone who already knew the text of the Book of Abraham could have it brought to mind by reading a seemingly unrelated text, the Book of Breathings Made by Isis. This theory has been widely misunderstood and misinterpreted as a theory dealing with the relationship of the papyri to the Book of Abraham. The authors of this theory, however, do not argue that Joseph Smith used this correlation to produce the Book of Abraham, but that someone in ancient times used this as a means to recall a memorized text.

Nature of the Facsimiles

The Book of Abraham is unique in Latter-day Saint scripture because ancient illustrations accompany the text. Perhaps no aspect of the Book of Abraham has provoked more controversy or comment than its facsimiles. There have been several attempts to explain the facsimiles and their relationship to the Book of Abraham.

The major non-Mormon theory is that the facsimiles belong to Egyptian funerary texts and have nothing whatsoever to do with Abraham. Proponents of this theory support it using one of four major arguments: (1) Because Facsimiles 1 and 3 of the Book of Abraham were on the same roll as the so-called Book of Breathings Made by Isis, these facsimiles must derive from the Book of Breathings Made by Isis; (2) the facsimiles are typical vignettes from the Book of the Dead; (3) the elements in the facsimiles are common elements found in vignettes from the Book of the Dead; or (4) the facsimiles are common funerary vignettes. These arguments are not necessarily compatible.

There are problems with each of these arguments: (1) Arguing that Facsimiles 1 and 3 are part of the so-called Book of Breathings Made by Isis fails to explain why no other copy of this book has vignettes similar to the facsimiles. (2) Those who argue that the facsimiles are typical vignettes from the Book of the Dead fail to produce parallel vignettes from said book, which is strange if they occur so often. Supposedly parallel vignettes usually lack significant elements found in the facsimiles or contain significant elements that the facsimiles lack. (3) Those who argue that elements in the facsimiles are commonly found in vignettes from the Book of the Dead often fail to provide specific examples from the Book of the Dead. For example, while canopic jars are occasionally depicted on copies of the Book of the Dead, they are not common. (4) Although widening the scope to include any funerary vignettes results in parallels to Facsimile 2, it has so far not produced parallels to Facsimiles 1 or 3. Most of the known parallels to Facsimile 1 are from temple contexts, not funerary contexts, and those who point to these parallels fail to pay attention both to important differences between the parallels and Facsimile 1 or to the context of the supposed parallels. Most of the collections of parallels to Facsimile 2 are incomplete, and those who point to these parallels usually ignore the identifications of the individual figures in the Egyptian inscriptions.

The second theory is that the facsimiles originated with Abraham and were drawn by him on the papyrus. This approach assumes that the papyri date to Abraham's day. Problems exist with this theory as well: if the papyri date to later than Abraham, the artwork cannot have been Abraham's. In support of a later date, the artwork of the facsimiles is not in the style of Abraham's day.

A third theory is that the facsimiles originated with Abraham and were copied along with the manuscript. (We should not assume that the ancient scribes even attempted to copy the facsimiles with photographic accuracy.) This theory has the advantage of being able to explain the style of the vignettes but has the disadvantage of largely being neither provable nor disprovable.

A fourth theory is that the facsimiles are illustrations only loosely dependent on the text. They are illustrations of the time period in which the papyri were produced, using stock motifs of the art of that time and place. The facsimiles thus are comparable to medieval manuscript illuminations. This theory has the advantage of matching the way Egyptian vignettes were produced.

Joseph Smith Papyrus IV (in current condition). This fragment, from a papyrus originally belonging to a woman named Semminis, contains text and vignettes from Book of the Dead chapters 91, 100, 101, 103, 104, 105, and 106. In the nineteenth century, fragments from other papyri were glued in to patch holes.

4

The Facsimiles of the Book of Abraham

The facsimiles of the Book of Abraham and their interpretation have sparked considerable discussion. We may divide these into discussions over the copying and interpretation of the facsimiles.

There is some evidence to indicate that the papyri containing the facsimiles of the Book of Abraham were already damaged when Joseph Smith obtained them. The original of Facsimile 1 is now in bad condition with many missing areas, and much debate has focused on guessing how much of the damage occurred after Joseph Smith owned the papyrus. A sketch of Facsimile 2 made in 1842, probably by Willard Richards, shows areas of that facsimile that were damaged. Facsimile 3 was apparently destroyed in the Chicago Fire but seems to have been largely intact when Joseph Smith had it.

The original facsimiles were engraved to size by Reuben Hedlock in 1842. Comparison of the remaining portions of Joseph Smith Papyrus I with the original publication of Facsimile 1 shows that Hedlock produced a careful, faithful—though not entirely photographically accurate—copy of the papyrus. Later versions of the facsimiles were not as carefully copied as Hedlock's. The most inaccurate versions of the facsimiles were originally published in the 1907 edition of the Pearl of Great Price and perpetuated until the 1981 edition, which returned to Hedlock's engraving (see chart on page 7). Unfortunately, many Egyptological publications, contrary to their normal epigraphic standards, continue to use the 1907 edition of the facsimiles instead of the 1842 or 1981 edition.

It has been constant practice to compare and contrast Joseph Smith's explanations of the facsimiles with those of modern Egyptologists. Joseph Smith's "explanations" (found on the adjoining pages in the Pearl of Great Price) are short statements that serve as a key to identify the figures. The use of the facsimiles as illustrations of the Book of Abraham is dependent on the text of the Book of Abraham. Only the subject illustrated by Facsimile 1 corresponds with the text of the Book of Abraham; the other facsimiles correspond to portions of the Book of Abraham that were not published. Egyptological interpretations of the facsimiles begin with the assumption that the facsimiles are standard illustrations for funerary texts. These interpretations are often hampered by the lack of good recent Egyptological studies of the class of illustrations to which the various facsimiles belong. Comparisons between Joseph Smith's explanations and those of the ancient Egyptians are generally hampered by insufficient attention to the prob-

A Brief Outline of the Contents of the Book of Abraham

The following is an overview of the contents of the Book of Abraham. Although Joseph Smith did not publish the entire Book of Abraham, some of the contents may be inferred from the facsimiles and other statements in the Book of Abraham; these inferences are placed in square brackets.

1. Abraham in Ur of the Chaldees (see Abraham 1:1–2:4)
    a. Sacrifice of Abraham (see Abraham 1:5–20)
    b. Egyptian History of Abraham's day (see Abraham 1:20–28)
2. Abraham's Travels in Syria and Canaan (see Abraham 2:4–?)
    a. Abrahamic Covenant (see Abraham 2:6–13)
    b. Abraham's Travels in Canaan (see Abraham 2:14–21)
    c. Sacrifice of Sarah (see Abraham 2:21–25)
    d. Abraham's Vision (see Abraham 3:1–5:21)
        i. Astronomy Lesson (see Abraham 3:1–19)
        ii. Premortal existence (see Abraham 3:20–28)
        iii. Creation (see Abraham 4:1–5:21)
        iv. [Fall] (inferred from Abraham 1:31)
    e. [Nature of the Cosmos] (inferred from Abraham 1:31; Facsimile 2)
3. [Travels in Egypt] (implied in Abraham 2:21–22, Facsimile 3)
    a. [Abraham in Pharaoh's court] (Facsimile 3)

lems involved in such comparisons: (1) We only know what Joseph Smith called the figures in the facsimiles, but we do not have corresponding portions of the Book of Abraham that would tell the story portrayed in two of the facsimiles. (2) Some individuals have paid insufficient attention to the evidence of what the Egyptians thought the facsimiles meant. In comparing Joseph Smith's understanding of the facsimiles with ancient Egyptian understanding of the facsimiles, we are comparing two unknowns. While some (but not all) studies by Latter-day Saints have been overeager to find similarities between Joseph Smith's explanations of various figures and those of Egyptologists, studies by critics have generally been unwilling to grant that Joseph Smith could have gotten anything correct, even by coincidence. Additionally, most studies of the facsimiles (whether looking at Joseph Smith's or ancient Egyptian interpretations) have suffered from merely identifying the parts without exploring how those parts interact to form a whole.

While it would be impossible to briefly summarize the debate on the facsimiles, the principal issues relating to each of the facsimiles have been as follows:

Facsimile 1: Every figure in this facsimile has been discussed somewhere. Because the papyrus in its

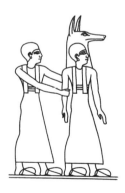

Right: Ptolemaic period drawing from the temple of Dendara depicting priests as both being bald and wearing jackal masks. Left: Example of such a mask (with eyeholes) now in the collection of the Römer und Pelizaeus Museum in Hildesheim, Germany.

Facsimile 1 of the Book of Abraham.

present state is not as complete as Facsimile 1, however, controversy here has focused on whether the heads of figures 1 and 3 have been restored correctly, whether there was a knife in the hand of figure 3, and whether figure 2 had two hands or one. Some have argued that figure 1 should have a human head and figure 3 should have a jackal's head. A variety of restorations have been suggested for figure 2, usually replacing one of the hands with a bird (even though Egyptians at that time period did not draw birds' wings that way; see chart on page 38) and replacing the knife with some other object, varying from the innocuous to the obscene. The discussion about figure 3 has cen-

Wing or Hand?

Wings

JSP VI. Typical wing feathers are outlined.

Book of the Dead 89 from P. Turin. No feathers are indicated.

Book of the Dead 157 from P. Turin. Another typical wing.

JSP IV. Feathers go down, not out.

JSP I

Hands

JSP IV. Note how the thumbs are outlined.

JSP I. Note that the wing is not drawn the same way as the hands.

Strokes used in making JSP I.

The two hands superimposed on each other.

Because Joseph Smith Papyrus I currently has a hole where the arms should be, some have suggested that the upper ink traces are those of a wing rather than a hand. A hand, however, is the only possibility—first because wings were not drawn that way at the time the papyrus was made, and second because of the clear thumb stroke at the bottom of both hands, which is not characteristic of a wing. So similar are the two hands that they can easily be superimposed one on top of the other. Neither hand resembles the adjacent wing.

Facsimile 2 of the Book of Abraham.

tered on whether the head should be that of a jackal or a bald man. Whether the head is a jackal or a bald man in no way affects the interpretation of the figure, however, since in either case the figure would be a priest.[13] The presence of a knife in the hand of figure 3, while unusual, is attested by certain observers when the papyri were still intact and by one observer before Facsimile 1 was made.[14] Issues concerning the accuracy of both the artwork and the copying are routinely clouded by shifting the responsibility of the artwork from the engraver, Reuben Hedlock, to Joseph Smith, without adducing any evidence to identify a particular individual with the responsibility for the restorations.

Facsimile 2: This facsimile has attracted much attention

Figure 7 from Cairo CG 9446, the only known ancient Egyptian identification of figure 7 on a hypocephalus: "the great god."

because of its round shape and complicated Greek name, hypocephalus. Nearly every figure in this facsimile has been discussed in various places, with arguments for and against the explanations provided. Joseph Smith's identification of figure 6 as the four quarters of the earth finds substantiation in Egyptological literature.[15] Some have focused attention on how figure 3 (God sitting upon his throne) is drawn as though it were out of place, but they fail to acknowledge that the figure finds parallels in several hypocephali. Certain sectarians have also focused on the identification of figure 7 (God sitting upon his throne), although their normal identification of that figure finds no support in any known hypocephali: the only known ancient Egyptian identification of figure 7 is "the great god."[16] Although it is generally acknowledged that there is a connection between hypocephali and Book of the Dead chapter 162, the specific relationships remain inadequately explored.

Facsimile 3: Facsimile 3 has received the least attention. The principal complaint raised by the critics has been regarding the female attire worn by figures 2 and 4, who are identified as male royalty. It has been documented, however, that on certain occasions, for certain ritual purposes, some Egyptian men dressed up as women.[17]

Facsimile 3 of the Book of Abraham.

Left: **Joseph Smith Papyrus VI**. Right: **Joseph Smith Papyrus V** (both in current condition). These fragments, from a papyrus originally owned by Semminis (a woman from the third century B.C.), contain text and vignettes from Book of the Dead chapters 72, 74, 75, 76, 77, 83, 86, 87, 88, 89.

5

The Role of the Book of Abraham in Latter-day Saint Scripture

When discussing the Book of Abraham, non–Latter-day Saints generally take no cognizance of the role the Book of Abraham plays in the tradition of Latter-day Saint scripture. They ignore why Latter-day Saints think the Book of Abraham is important and concentrate on aspects that have little or no relevance to Latter-day Saints.

For example, one of the claims is that the Book of Abraham is used primarily to sanction bigotry. A close reading of the text, however, does not sustain such contentions. Furthermore, Latter-day Saints do not use the text in this fashion.

One of the important uses of the Book of Abraham by Latter-day Saints is its particular

wording of the Abrahamic covenant. This wording clarifies how Abraham's seed will bless "all the families of the earth" (Abraham 2:11).

The largest effect that the Book of Abraham has had on Latter-day Saint thought is its concept of the premortal existence and the purpose of life. Although other Latter-day Saint scriptures discuss the premortal existence, the Book of Abraham provides the clearest explanation of this key Latter-day Saint doctrine. The Book of Abraham explains that God organized all the spirits of this world "before this world was" (Abraham 3:22), explained its purpose (see Abraham 3:24), and stated that this earthly existence was to "prove them herewith, to see if they will do all things whatsoever the Lord their God shall command them" (Abraham 3:25).

The issues discussed in this guide have little if any relevance to most Latter-day Saints in their acceptance or use of the Book of Abraham. To Latter-day Saints, the contents of the Book of Abraham are far more important than the contents of the remaining fragments of the Joseph Smith Papyri.

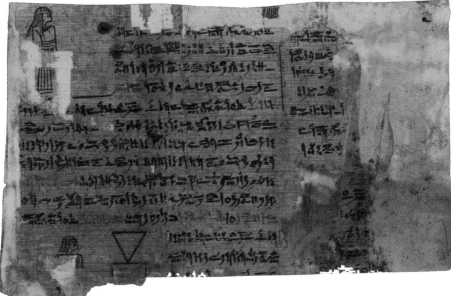

Above: **Joseph Smith Papyrus VII**. Below: **Joseph Smith Papyrus VIII** (both in current condition). These fragments, from a papyrus originally belonging to a woman named Semminis, contain text and vignettes from Book of the Dead chapters 53, 54, 57, 63, 65, 67, 70.

6

Further Reading

Much of the basic work on the Book of Abraham remains to be done, but the following are the most important or original works.

19th- and 20th-Century History of the Papyri

Jay M. Todd, *The Saga of the Book of Abraham* (Salt Lake City: Deseret Book, 1969).

H. Donl Peterson, *The Story of the Book of Abraham: Mummies, Manuscripts, and Mormonism* (Salt Lake City: Deseret Book, 1995).

Brian L. Smith, "A Book of Abraham Research Update," *BYU Religious Studies Center Newsletter,* May 1997, 5–8.

John Gee, "A History of the Joseph Smith Papyri and Book of Abraham" (Provo, Utah: FARMS, 1999).

Editions of the Joseph Smith Papyri

"New Light on Joseph Smith's Egyptian Papyri," *Improvement Era* 71/2 (1968): 40–40i.

Hugh W. Nibley, *The Message of the Joseph Smith Papyri: An Egyptian Endowment* (Salt Lake City: Deseret Book, 1975).

Size of the JSP and Translation of the Book of Abraham

Hugh W. Nibley, "Judging and Prejudging the Book of Abraham" (Provo, Utah: FARMS, 1984).

John Gee, "A History of the Joseph Smith Papyri and Book of Abraham" (Provo, Utah: FARMS, 1999).

John Gee, "Eyewitness, Hearsay, and Physical Evidence of the Joseph Smith Papyri," in *The Disciple as Witness: Essays on Latter-day Saint History and Doctrine in Honor of Richard Lloyd Anderson* (Provo, Utah: FARMS, 2000), 175–217.

Ancient Background of the Joseph Smith Papyri

Hugh W. Nibley, *The Message of the Joseph Smith Papyri: An Egyptian Endowment* (Salt Lake City: Deseret Book, 1975).

John Gee, "Abraham in Ancient Egyptian Texts," *Ensign*, July 1992, 60–62.

John Gee, "Abracadabra, Isaac, and Jacob," *Review of Books on the Book of Mormon* 7/1 (1995): 19–84.

John Gee, "The Ancient Owners of the Joseph Smith Papyri" (Provo, Utah: FARMS, 1999).

Role of the Book of Abraham in Latter-day Saint Thought

John Gee, "The Role of the Book of Abraham in the Restoration" (Provo, Utah: FARMS, 1997).

Facsimiles of the Book of Abraham

Michael D. Rhodes, "A Translation and Commentary of the Joseph Smith Hypocephalus," *BYU Studies* 17/3 (1977): 259–74.

Michael D. Rhodes, "The Joseph Smith Hypocephalus . . . Seventeen Years Later" (Provo, Utah: FARMS, 1994).

Abrahamic Background of the Book of Abraham

Hugh W. Nibley, "A New Look at the Pearl of Great Price," *Improvement Era* 71/1–73/5 (January 1968–May 1970); reprinted as a booklet (Provo, Utah: FARMS).

John A. Tvedtnes, "The Location of Abraham's Birthplace and the Original Homeland of the Hebrews," in *Ur of the Chaldeans: Increasing Evidence on the Birthplace of Abraham and the Original Homeland of the Hebrews* (Provo, Utah: Society for Early Historic Archaeology, 1985), 8–42.

Paul Y. Hoskisson, "Where Was Ur of the Chaldees?" in *The Pearl of Great Price: Revelations from God*, ed. H. Donl Peterson and Charles D. Tate Jr. (Provo, Utah: BYU Religious Studies Center, 1989), 119–36.

Daniel C. Peterson, "News from Antiquity," *Ensign*, January 1994, 16–21.

Hugh W. Nibley, *Abraham in Egypt*, 2nd ed. (Salt Lake City: Deseret Book and FARMS, 2000).

John Gee and Stephen D. Ricks, "Historical Plausibility: The Book of Abraham as a Case Study," in *Historicity and the Latter-day Saint Scriptures*, ed. Paul Y. Hoskisson (Provo, Utah: BYU Religious Studies Center, forthcoming).

John A. Tvedtnes, Brian M. Hauglid, and John Gee, *Early Traditions about Abraham Relevant to a Study of the Book of Abraham* (Provo, Utah: FARMS, forthcoming).

Joseph Smith Papyrus IX (in current condition). These fragments, from a papyrus originally owned by a woman named Semminis, contain text from Book of the Dead chapters 3, 4, 5, 6, 65, 125, and other unidentified texts and vignettes.

Glossary
of Names

Abraham was an ancient biblical patriarch. Jews, Christians, and Muslims view him as the father of the faithful. Born in Ur of the Chaldees, Abraham moved to Haran, the land of Canaan, and Egypt before returning to Canaan. He is most noted for his faith in, obedience to, and covenant with God.

Amenophis *(imn-ḥtp)*, son of Tanoub, was an Egyptian priest at Thebes during the Ptolemaic period (332–30 B.C.). A papyrus belonging to him was in Joseph Smith's possession but has since been lost (see pp. 10–13, 59).

Simeon Andrews (1798–?) was a farmer in Kirtland. He contributed $800 toward the purchase of the mummies and the Joseph Smith Papyri when Joseph Smith purchased them in July 1835. He moved to Nauvoo and later traveled west to Utah in 1847. In 1851 he served as a counselor in the California Branch (see pp. 2, 3).

Artapanus was a Jewish author who lived in Egypt before the first century B.C., probably during the reign of Ptolemy V. Artapanus mentioned Abraham in his works, noting that he taught astronomy to the Egyptians (see p. 16).

Lewis C. Bidamon (1806–1891), never a member of the Church of Jesus Christ of Latter-day Saints, moved to Nauvoo in 1846 and married Emma Smith in 1847. With Emma and Joseph Smith III, Bidamon sold the Joseph Smith Papyri and mummies to Abel Combs in May 1856 (see pp. 2, 9, 57).

Ludlow Bull (1886–1954) was an American Egyptologist. Originally educated in law, he left his legal practice to study Egyptology, receiving his Ph.D. in 1922. He started the Egyptology program at Yale and was an associate curator for the Metropolitan Museum of Art's Department of Egyptian Art. Bull acquired the Joseph Smith Papyri for the museum toward the end of his tenure (see p. 9).

Michael H. Chandler (1797–1866) was born in Ireland. Living in New York in 1833, he borrowed $6000 to buy eleven mummies containing several papyrus manuscripts, now known as the Joseph Smith Papyri. Chandler toured the U.S. exhibiting the mummies, selling seven of them along the way. In 1835 he sold the remaining four mummies and the papyri to Joseph Smith for $2400. The account Chandler gave the Mormons of the mummies and papyri contains many inaccuracies, exaggerations, and fabrications, as well as some truth (see pp. 1, 2, 5).

Chibois (*tꜣy-ḥy-biꜣ.t*) was the wife of Osoroeris and mother of Hor. She lived at the end of the third century B.C. The name Chibois was common in Ptolemaic Egypt and is mentioned in a number of documents, none of which can be assigned to her with any certainty (see pp. 11, 54).

Joseph Coe (1774–1854) was baptized a member of the Church of Jesus Christ of Latter-day Saints in 1831. He was appointed as an agent to purchase church property in 1833, and in 1835 assisted in purchasing the mummies and papyri. Coe left the church in 1838 in Ohio (see pp. 2, 3).

Abel Combs (1823–1892) was a farmer, plater, lampmaker, latherer, machinist, and artist from Ohio. Combs left Ohio in 1855 and traveled to the Midwest. He purchased the Joseph Smith Papyri and the accompanying mummies in 1856 in Nauvoo, selling some of the antiquities almost immediately to the St. Louis Museum (see pp. 2, 9, 52, 55, 57, 58).

Oliver Cowdery (1806–1850) was a teacher, lawyer, and newspaper editor. After serving as a school teacher in Palmyra, New York, he acted as scribe to Joseph Smith for the translation of the Book of Mormon. He was one of the Three Witnesses to the Book of Mormon, seeing both the plates from which they were translated and the angel; he was also present at a number of divine visitations. One of the first elders of the Church of Jesus Christ of Latter-day Saints at its organization in 1830, Cowdery was appointed assistant president of the church in 1834. He left the church in 1838 in Missouri and then worked as a lawyer in Ohio and Wisconsin. In 1848 Oliver Cowdery was rebaptized into the church (see p. 5).

Eskhons (*ns-ḫnsw*), mother of Semminis. Nothing else is known about her at this time, other than that she lived in the late third century B.C. (see pp. 11, 56).

Eupolemus was a Jew (or perhaps a Samaritan) who lived in the mid–second century B.C. In one of his writings he claimed that Abraham taught the Egyptians astronomy (see p. 16).

Hecataeus of Abdera lived in the time of the Egyptian king Ptolemy I (about 300 B.C.). When Ptolemy I controlled Abdera, Hecataeus traveled to Egypt, going as far south as Thebes to learn about Egypt firsthand. Five books are attributed to Hecataeus, including *Concerning the Jews* and *About Abraham and the Egyptians.* Only a fragment of the latter work is preserved, but it mentions Abraham teaching the Egyptians astronomy (see p. 16).

Reuben Hedlock (1801–?) was a carpenter in Ohio. After joining the church, he was appointed as the president of the quorum of elders in Kirtland, Ohio, in 1837 but moved to Missouri in 1838. He served a mission in England in 1840, returning to Nauvoo the next year. He prepared the facsimiles for the publication of the Book of Abraham in 1842. In 1843 he returned to England to preside over that mission until he was excommunicated in 1845 (see pp. 4, 5, 6, 7, 34, 39).

Alice Combs Weaver Heusser inherited the Joseph Smith Papyri from her mother, Charlotte Weaver. Alice married Edward Heusser in 1896. She approached the Metropolitan Museum of Art to sell the papyri in 1918, but they were not interested at the time, so she kept the papyri until her death (see pp. 2, 9).

Edward Heusser married Alice Combs Weaver in 1896. He sold the Joseph Smith Papyri to the Metropolitan Museum of Art in 1947 (see pp. 2, 9).

Hor *(ḥr),* son of Osoroeris and Chibois, held the offices of prophet of Amonrasonter, prophet of Min-who-massacres-his-enemies, and prophet of Chespisichis in Thebes at the beginning of the second century B.C. He is known to have had at least two sons, Osoroeris and

Harsiesis. He was the original owner of Joseph Smith Papyri I, X, and XI (see pp. 10–13, 15, 60).

Charlotte E. Benecke Weaver Huntsman was a nurse to Abel Combs and acquired the Joseph Smith Papyri from him, which she later passed to her daughter (see pp. 2, 9, 54).

Giovanni Pietro Antonio Lebolo (1781–1830) was born in Castellamonte, Italy. He enrolled in Napoleon's army in 1799 and was injured in 1801 at San Agostino. After the defeat of Napoleon, Lebolo went to Egypt and worked for Bernardino Drovetti (former French consul general to Egypt) between 1817 and 1822, during which time he excavated the mummies with which the Joseph Smith Papyri were buried and also the Soter family tomb. He returned to Italy in 1822, settling in Castellamonte in 1825, and went into the grocery and real estate businesses (see pp. 1, 2, 25, 59, 64).

Noufianoub *(nfr-ir.t-nbw)*. Her name is attested only as the owner of Joseph Smith Papyrus III. She was a wealthy Egyptian living in the area of Thebes during the Ptolemaic period (332–30 B.C.) (see pp. 10–13, 18).

Albano Oblasser was an Italian shipper based in Trieste. Antonio Lebolo sent the mummies and the Joseph Smith Papyri through Oblasser to New York to be sold in the late 1820s or early 1830s (see pp. 1, 2).

Osoroeris *(wsir-wr)*, son of Chaponchonsis and father of Hor, held the offices of prophet of Amonrasonter, prophet of Min-who-massacres-his-enemies, prophet of Chespisichis, keeper of secrets, and other priestly offices. He was also the great governor in Thebes at the end of the third century B.C. (see pp. 11, 15, 52, 54).

Warren Parrish (1803–1887) was baptized into the Church of Jesus Christ of Latter-day Saints in May 1833 by Brigham

Young. From 1834 to 1835 he served a mission in Kentucky and Tennessee with Wilford Woodruff. Parrish was a scribe to Joseph Smith from 29 October 1835 to April 1836 and assisted in the translation of the Book of Abraham after April 1836. In 1837 he renounced his church membership and was unsuccessful in leading a splinter group. In 1850 he was a clergyman in Mendon, New York. At his death he was classified as insane (see pp. 4, 5).

Josiah Quincy (1802–1882) became mayor of Boston in 1845. He visited Nauvoo in 1844 and was shown the Joseph Smith Papyri. Quincy left an account of what he saw, which appears accurate, but records of others who were present show that many of his statements about what he heard are inaccurate (see pp. 25, 65).

Franklin D. Richards (1821–1899) was ordained an apostle of the church on 12 February 1849. He presided over the European Mission from 1851 to 1852, where he published the Pearl of Great Price in England in 1851. Richards became president of the Quorum of the Twelve Apostles in 1898 (see p. 6).

Willard Richards (1804–1854) was a medical doctor who converted to the Church of Jesus Christ of Latter-day Saints in December 1836. From 1837 to 1841 he served a mission in England. Richards was ordained an apostle in 1840. He served as a private secretary to Joseph Smith from 1841 to 1844 and was with Joseph Smith when he was assassinated. In 1847 Richards moved to Utah with the Mormon pioneers (see pp. 4, 33).

Semminis (*t₃-šr.t-mn*), daughter of Eskhons, was a wealthy Egyptian apparently of priestly lineage in the late third century B.C. She owned Joseph Smith Papyri II, IV, V, VI, VII, VIII, and IX (see pp. 10–13, 14, 32, 42, 46, 50).

Sesonchis (or **Sheshonq**) *(ššnq)* was a wealthy member of an Egyptian priestly family. He owned the original hypocephalus of which Facsimile 2 is a copy. The name Sesonchis was common in Egypt, and without further information it would be impossible to identify the owner of the Joseph Smith hypocephalus with any other known Sesonchis (see p. 11).

Emma Hale Smith (1804–1879) married Joseph Smith Jr. in 1827. She assisted her husband as a scribe during the translation of the Book of Mormon and was allowed to handle the plates from which it was translated, although she never saw them. Emma was baptized a member of the Church of Jesus Christ of Latter-day Saints in 1830. In 1835 she helped compile the first hymnal, and in 1842 she was appointed the first president of the Female Relief Society in Nauvoo, Illinois. She remained in Nauvoo after the death of her husband in 1844. In 1847 she married Lewis C. Bidamon and, with him and her son Joseph Smith III, sold the Joseph Smith Papyri to Abel Combs in 1856 (see pp. 2, 9, 52, 58).

Joseph Smith Jr. (1805–1844) received his first divine vision in 1820. In 1829 he translated the Book of Mormon from gold plates. He organized the Church of Jesus Christ of Latter-day Saints on 6 April 1830, becoming its first prophet and president. From 1830 to 1833 he worked on a translation of the Bible. He acquired a number of papyrus documents and mummies in July 1835 and translated the Book of Abraham later in the month, publishing it in 1842. Driven from New York in 1831, he settled in Ohio, journeying frequently to Missouri, until he moved there in 1838. Under threat of extermination by the Missouri government, the Mormons left Missouri and settled in

Illinois, where Joseph Smith founded the city of Nauvoo. In 1842 he was elected mayor of Nauvoo, and in 1844 he ran for President of the United States. He was assassinated by a mob in Carthage, Illinois, on 27 June 1844.

Joseph Smith III (1832–1914) was still a young boy when his father, Joseph Smith Jr., was killed. In 1856 he sold the mummies and Joseph Smith Papyri to Abel Combs. In 1860 he became president of the Reorganized Church of Jesus Christ of Latter Day Saints (see pp. 2, 9, 52, 57).

Lucy Mack Smith (1775–1856) was the wife of Joseph Smith Sr. and mother of the Prophet Joseph Smith Jr. She was baptized a member of the Church of Jesus Christ of Latter-day Saints in 1830 and wrote a biographical sketch of her son in 1845. Widowed in 1840 and preceded in death by most of her children, Lucy remained in Nauvoo after the death of Joseph Smith Jr., in the care of his wife Emma. Lucy Mack Smith retained possession of the Joseph Smith Papyri after her son's death until her own death in 1856 (see pp. 2, 9).

Philo of Alexandria (30 B.C.–A.D. 45) was a Jewish priest who lived in Alexandria, Egypt, at the time of Trajan in the first century A.D. He was steeped in both Jewish lore and Greek philosophy. Philo interpreted the Bible allegorically to show that the Bible really taught the then-trendy scholarly philosophy Middle Platonism. Philo used nonbiblical traditions to support his allegorical interpretation, including several that dealt with Abraham and his knowledge of astronomy (see p. 16).

Soter, son of Cornelius Pollus, was archon of Thebes in A.D. 107. His family was prominent in Thebes and quite wealthy. The Soter family coffins, excavated by Antonio Lebolo, are a major source of astronomical material from Roman-period Egypt (see pp. 26, 27, 55, 64).

Tanoub *(t3-nbw)* was the mother of Amenophis and presumably lived in the Ptolemaic period (332–30 B.C). There were many people by the name of Tanoub in Ptolemaic Thebes, but it is not certain which of these she may have been (see pp. 11, 51).

Zosimus of Panopolis was an Egyptian alchemist who lived in the third century A.D. He draws on both Jewish and Egyptian sources in his alchemical work, some of which has survived (see p. 16).

Above: **Joseph Smith Papyrus X**. Below: **Joseph Smith Papyrus XI** (both in current condition). These papyri contain four of six columns of the Book of Breathings Made by Isis and comprise the oldest known copy of this text.

Glossary
of Terms

Anastasi archive: A collection of documents from a temple archive containing material in hieratic, demotic, Old Coptic (a form of Egyptian written in Greek characters), and Greek. Using paleography, the archive has been dated to the second through fourth centuries A.D. The archive contains material on alchemy and literature, but most of the manuscripts are manuals that describe Egyptian rituals. Abraham is mentioned in a number of places in the archive in the context of lion couches, hypocephali, and astronomy. The collection takes its name from Giovanni d'Anastasi, an Egyptian antiquities collector of the early nineteenth century (see p. 16).

Book of Breathings: A large number of documents are classified under this heading. The modern title derives from the Egyp-

tian title which, because of multiple meanings, can be literally translated as either "Book of Breathings" or "Letter of Fellowship." Books of Breathings have been classified in many ways in the past, but the current classification, based on ancient titles, is as follows: Book of Breathings Made by Isis (formerly called the First Book of Breathings), First Book of Breathings (formerly called the Second Book of Breathings type II, a and b), and Second Book of Breathings (formerly called the Second Book of Breathings type IV). Other Books of Breathings are known and vary in content (see pp. 10, 28, 29).

Book of the Dead: A collection of ancient Egyptian religious texts called (in Egyptian) The Book of Going Forth by Day. It has its modern designation because copies are typically found buried with dead individuals. Although some of the chapters have a specific funerary function, other chapters were used for religious purposes while the individual was still alive. The contents of the chapters are often incomprehensible to modern readers, even Egyptologists. Until Saite times (after about 672 B.C.), the contents of the Book of the Dead were neither standardized in the selection of chapters nor in their ordering (see pp. 10, 26, 29, 40, 64).

canopic jars: Stone or ceramic jars originally designed to contain the internal organs of mummies. Originally the jars had plain stoppers (lids). Later, during the First Intermediate Period (2200–2040 B.C.), the stoppers were shaped as human heads. Eventually, by the end of the Eighteenth Dynasty (about 1300 B.C.), the jars' lids resembled animal heads. Ultimately (about 500 B.C.), the jars merely functioned as decoration and even ceased to be hollowed out.

Figures 5–8 of Facsimile 1 of the Book of Abraham are canopic jars, though they are shaped like those that were not hollowed out (see p. 29).

demotic: An Egyptian script that developed out of hieratic (see *hieratic* below) that was used for business documents in the Nile Delta region. The earliest dated example comes from 657 B.C. and the latest comes from A.D. 457, over a century after Christianity became the official religion of Egypt (see pp. 26, 61).

facsimile: A reproduction or copy of a manuscript. The Book of Abraham included three facsimiles of the vignettes (see *vignette* below) from Egyptian manuscripts.

hieratic: Originally a cursive form of hieroglyphs, this Egyptian script was first attested at the beginning of the early dynastic period (about 3100 B.C.). It continued to be used until the third century A.D. While hieroglyphs were most often used for carving, hieratic was used mainly for brush and ink on papyrus, although it appears on other surfaces as well. Most of the Joseph Smith Papyri were written in hieratic (see pp. 25, 27, 61).

hypocephalus: Derived from Greek terms meaning "under the head," the term *hypocephalus* (plural, *hypocephali*) is used for illustrated circular devices placed under the back of the head or atop the crown of mummies. The earliest known examples date to Saite times (672–525 B.C.) while the latest examples date to the Ptolemaic period (332–30 B.C.). Hypocephali were supposed to be made of gold, but most only imitate gold. Although normally associated with Book of the Dead chapter 162, a variety of texts and scenes can appear on hypocephali (see pp. 7, 10, 12, 39, 49, 57, 61).

paleography: The art of dating manuscripts according to handwriting style (see p. 61).

Septuagint (LXX): A translation of the Hebrew Bible (or Old Testament) made into Greek in Egypt, supposedly at the request of Ptolemy II Philadelphos. Almost three hundred manuscripts of the Septuagint have been found at numerous places in Egypt, including Thebes, Oxyrhynchus, Memphis, and Elephantine, and subsequently published (see p. 16).

Soter find: A group of objects originally belonging to the family of Soter, who was archon of Thebes in A.D. 107. Because these objects were dug up by Antonio Lebolo, some people have thought they might be connected to the Joseph Smith Papyri (see pp. 25, 27).

Testament of Abraham: A noncanonical work that deals with Abraham's visions of the cosmos and the purpose of life just before his death. It is generally thought to have been composed in Egypt in the first century A.D (see p. 16).

textual transmission: A term for how a manuscript is passed down or transmitted through time and space (see pp. 27–28).

vignette: A sketch or illustration located at the beginning or end of a section of text. Many such drawings accompany chapters of the Book of the Dead (pp. 10, 29, 30).

Notes

1. A more detailed account of the history of the papyri may be found in H. Donl Peterson, *The Story of the Book of Abraham: Mummies, Manuscripts, and Mormonism* (Salt Lake City: Deseret Book, 1995), 36–118.

2. *History of the Church of Jesus Christ of Latter-day Saints*, 2nd ed. (Salt Lake City: Deseret Book, 1950), 2:236.

3. For the price, see Peterson, *Story of the Book of Abraham*, 6–7. For the number of papyri, see John Gee, "A Tragedy of Errors," *Review of Books on the Book of Mormon* 4/1 (1992): 108–9.

4. See *History of the Church*, 2:253.

5. See ibid., 2:286.

6. Warren Parrish, letter to the editor, *Painesville Republican*, 15 February 1838, 3.

7. *The Pearl of Great Price* (Liverpool: F. D. Richards, 1851), title page.

8. Franklin D. Richards, "Preface" in *The Pearl of Great Price* (Liverpool: F. D. Richards, 1851), v.

9. See Peterson, *Story of the Book of Abraham*, 203–4.

10. See "New Light on Joseph Smith's Egyptian Papyri," *Improvement Era* 71/2 (1968): 40–41.

11. The information in this section is based on John Gee, "Eyewitness, Hearsay, and Physical Evidence of the Joseph Smith Papyri," in *The Disciple as Witness: Essays on Latter-day Saint History*

and Doctrine in Honor of Richard Lloyd Anderson (Provo, Utah: FARMS, 2000), 175–217.

12. This is shown by comparing the various accounts of Josiah Quincy's visit with what Joseph Smith published about the papyri; see John Gee, "Telling the Story of the Joseph Smith Papyri," *FARMS Review of Books* 8/2 (1996): 53; and Gee, "Eyewitness, Hearsay, and Physical Evidence," 194–95.

13. The argument for the identification runs as follows:

(1) Assume for the sake of argument that the head on Facsimile 1 Figure 3 is correct. What are the implications of the figure being a bald man? Shaving was a common feature of initiation into the priesthood from the Old Kingdom through the Roman period. Since "Complete shaving of the head was another mark of the male Isiac votary and priest" the bald figure would then be a priest.

(2) Assume on the other hand that the head on Facsimile 1 Figure 3 is that of a jackal, as was first suggested by Theodule Devéria. We have representations of priests wearing masks, one example of an actual mask, [and] literary accounts from non-Egyptians about Egyptian priests wearing masks. . . .

Thus, however the restoration is made, the individual shown in Facsimile 1 Figure 3 is a priest, and the entire question of which head should be on the figure is moot so far as identifying the figure is concerned. (John Gee, "Abracadabra, Isaac, and Jacob," *Review of Books on the Book of Mormon* 7/1 [1995]: 80–82)

14. In 1841, before the facsimiles were made, William I. Appleby described Joseph Smith Papyrus I thus: "There are likewise representations of an Altar erected, with a man bound and laid thereon, and

a Priest with a knife in his hand, standing at the foot, with a dove over the person bound on the Altar with several Idol gods standing around it" (Gee, "Eyewitness, Hearsay, and Physical Evidence," 184). In 1842 Reverend Henry Caswall described the same papyrus as containing "'the figure of a man lying on a table' accompanied by a 'man standing by him with a drawn knife'" (185).

15. See Ian Shaw and Paul Nicholson, *British Museum Dictionary of Ancient Egypt* (London: British Museum, 1995), 275.

16. Cairo CG 9446, in Georges Daressy, *Textes et dessins magiques* (Cairo: Institut Français d'Archéologie Orientale, 1903), 53, pl. 13.

17. More information on this will be forthcoming, but one readily available instance is recorded in Apuleius, *Metamorphoses* 11.8.

Illustration Credits

Maps by Rebecca Sterrett.

Illustrations on the following pages are © *Intellectual Reserve, Inc. Used by permission:* x, 14, 18, 22, 32, 37, 38, 39, 41, 42, 46, 50, 60.

Photograph on page 36, courtesy Römer und Pelizaeus Museum, Hildesheim, Germany.

Line drawing on page 36, from the temple of Dendara, redrawn by Michael Lyon from Auguste Mariette, *Dendérah* (Paris: Franck, 1870), 4:pl. 31.

Papyrus Turin drawings on page 38 from Richard Lepsius, *Das Todtenbuch der Ägypter nach dem hieroglyphischen Papyris in Turin* (Leipzig: Wigard, 1842), pls. XXXIII and LXXVI.

Illustration on page 40, redrawn by Michael Lyon from Georges Daressy, *Textes et dessins magiques* (Cairo: Institut Français d'Arch-éologie Orientale, 1903), 53, pl. 13.

Selected FARMS Publications

Ancient Texts and Mormon Studies
Romans 1: Notes and Reflections
Popol Vuh: The Mythic Sections

THE COLLECTED WORKS OF HUGH NIBLEY
(COPUBLISHED WITH DESERET BOOK COMPANY)

Old Testament and Related Studies
Enoch the Prophet
The World and the Prophets
Mormonism and Early Christianity
Lehi in the Desert; The World of the Jaredites; There Were Jaredites
An Approach to the Book of Mormon
Since Cumorah
The Prophetic Book of Mormon
Approaching Zion
The Ancient State
Tinkling Cymbals and Sounding Brass
Temple and Cosmos
Brother Brigham Challenges the Saints
Abraham in Egypt

PUBLISHED THROUGH RESEARCH PRESS

Images of Ancient America: Visualizing Book of Mormon Life
Chiasmus in Antiquity (reprint)
Chiasmus Bibliography

PUBLICATIONS OF THE FARMS CENTER FOR THE PRESERVATION OF ANCIENT RELIGIOUS TEXTS

Dead Sea Scrolls Electronic Reference Library
The Incoherence of the Philosophers
The Niche of Lights
The Philosophy of Illumination

The Foundation for Ancient Research and Mormon Studies

The Foundation for Ancient Research and Mormon Studies (FARMS) encourages and supports research and publication about the Book of Mormon: Another Testament of Jesus Christ and other ancient scriptures.

FARMS is a nonprofit, tax-exempt educational foundation affiliated with Brigham Young University. Its main research interests in the scriptures include ancient history, language, literature, culture, geography, politics, religion, and law. Although research on such subjects is of secondary importance when compared with the spiritual and eternal messages of the scriptures, solid scholarly research can supply certain kinds of useful information, even if only tentatively, concerning many significant and interesting questions about the ancient backgrounds, origins, composition, and meanings of scripture.

The work of the Foundation rests on the premise that the Book of Mormon and other scriptures were written by prophets of God. Belief in this premise—in the divinity of scripture—is a matter of faith. It is hoped that this information will help people to "come unto Christ" (Jacob 1:7) and to understand and take more seriously these ancient witnesses of the atonement of Jesus Christ, the Son of God.

FARMS publishes information about the Book of Mormon and other ancient scripture in the *Insights* newsletter, books and research papers, *FARMS Review of Books, Journal of Book of Mormon Studies,* reprints of published scholarly papers, and videos and audiotapes. FARMS also supports the preparation of the Collected Works of Hugh Nibley.

To facilitate the sharing of information, FARMS sponsors lectures, seminars, symposia, firesides, and radio and television broadcasts in which research findings are communicated to working scholars and to anyone interested in faithful, reliable information about the scriptures.

For more information about the Foundation and its activities, contact the FARMS office at 1-800-327-6715 or (801) 373-5111. You can also visit the FARMS Web site at http://farms.byu.edu.